SCIENCE C

Sound and Hearing

Angela Royston

Explore the world with **Popcorn** - your complete first non-fiction library.

Look out for more titles in the **Popcorn** range. All books have the same format of simple text and vibrant images. Text is carefully matched to the pictures to help readers to identify and understand key vocabulary.
www.waylandbooks.co.uk/popcorn

First published in 2010 by Wayland
Copyright © Wayland 2010

This paperback edition published in 2010 by Wayland

Wayland
338 Euston Road
London NW1 3BH

Wayland Australia
Level 17/207 Kent Street
Sydney NSW 2000

Editor: Katie Powell
Designer: Robert Walster
Picture Researcher: Diana Morris

British Library Cataloguing in Publication Data
Royston, Angela.
    Sound and hearing. -- (Popcorn. Science corner)
    1. Sound--Juvenile literature. 2. Hearing--Juvenile literature.
    I. Title II. Series
    534-dc22
ISBN 978 0 7502 6440 2

Printed and bound in China

Wayland is a division of Hachette Children's Books, an Hachette UK Company.
www.hachette.co.uk

Photographs:
Daniel Attia/Corbis: 8. Heide Benser/Corbis: 15. Bronwyn Photo/Shutterstock: 1, 7. Axel Ceschinski/Alamy: 20. Tim Cuff/Alamy: 19. Sam Diephius/Corbis: 18
Flying Colours/Getty Images: 13. Hoohooba/istockphoto: 10. Bob Jacobson/Corbis: 12. Slawomir Jastrzebski/istockphoto: 6. Michal Kakowiak/istockphoto: 5. Michael Matthews/Police Images/Alamy: 4. Cliff Parnell/istockphoto: front cover, 16. Thomas M Perkins/Shutterstock: 11. Aizar Raldes/Getty Images: 17. Tom Uhlenberg/Shutterstock: 2, 21. Wayland: 9, 14, 22, 23.

🔊 Contents

What is sound?

You hear a sound when something makes a noise. Different things make different kinds of noises.

Before you see an emergency vehicle, you might hear its siren.

You can tell which farm animal is making a noise from the sound it makes.

What noise does this animal make?

Hearing is one of your five senses. The other senses are seeing, smelling, tasting and touching.

How you hear

You hear when sounds travel to your ears. A noise makes tiny ripples in the air. They are like the ripples in a pond when raindrops fall onto the water.

The ripples are called sound waves.
Some of the sound waves go inside
your ears and your ears tell your brain
about the sounds.

Cupping your ear helps you to hear better.

You can
block out
a sound
by covering
your ears.

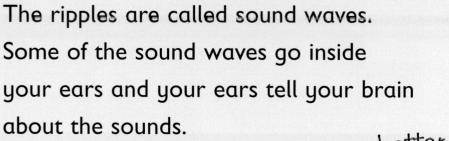

Making sounds

You can make sounds as well as hear them.
You use your voice to speak, shout and sing.
Clapping your hands or stamping your feet
makes a sound, too.

These girls are playing a clapping game.

One of the easiest ways to make a
sound is to bang two items together.

Tapping a saucepan
with a wooden spoon
makes a sound.

9

Musical instruments

Musical instruments make different sounds.
You play a piano by pressing the keys.

You play a drum by tapping the top of it with sticks, but you shake a tambourine.

You can bang a tambourine, too.

High and low sounds

A musical sound is called a note. Most musical instruments make high notes and low notes. The longest bar on this chime bar makes the lowest note.

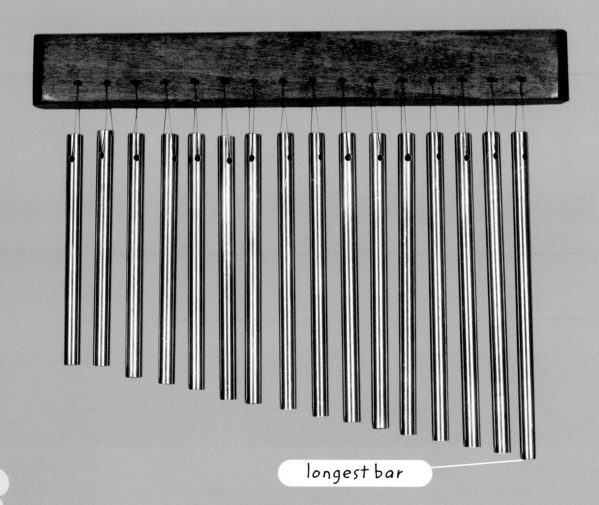

longest bar

The lowest sounds are made by the biggest instruments. A trumpet makes a lower sound than a flute.

trumpet

flute

Quiet sounds

Some sounds are so quiet you have to listen hard to hear them. You can whisper when you do not want people to hear what you are saying.

Tapping a drum gently with your
hand makes a very quiet sound.

Loud sounds

It takes a lot of effort to make a loud sound. It is harder to shout than to whisper.

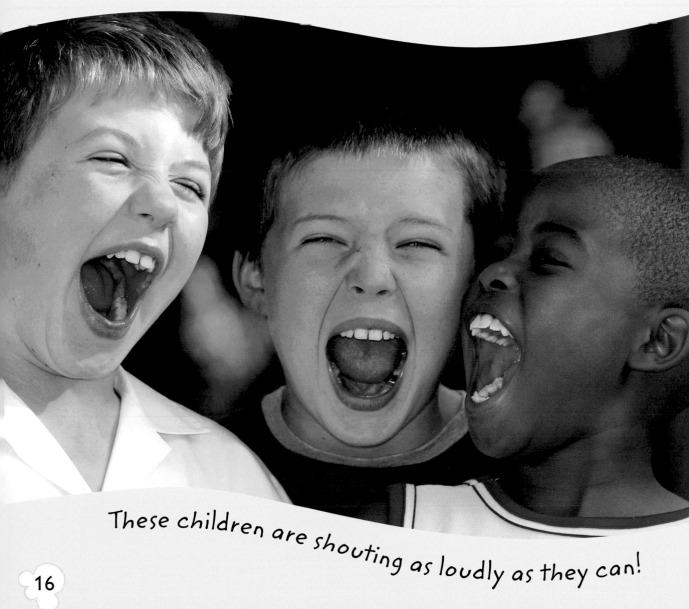

These children are shouting as loudly as they can!

The harder you bang a drum, the louder it will sound. If you smash two cymbals together they will make a loud noise!

Protect your hearing!

Very loud sounds can damage your ears.
If you like listening to music through headphones,
do not turn the sound up too loud.

Some machines are very noisy. People who work with these machines wear earmuffs to protect their hearing.

Warning!
Listening to very loud sounds can make you deaf as you get older.

Near or far

You can often tell how close a sound is by how loud it is. The closer you are to a noise, the louder it sounds.

When you are close to a cat, you can hear it purring.

As you move away from a sound, it becomes quieter. Very noisy things sound quiet when they are a long way away from you.

The sound of this aeroplane becomes quieter as it flies further away.

Make your own musical instruments

You will need:
- four empty plastic pots with lids
- rice
- uncooked pasta shapes
- sugar
- marbles

Follow these steps to make your own musical instruments.

1. Fill one of the pots half full with rice.

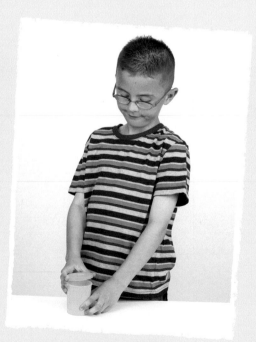

2. Put on the lid.

3. Use the pasta, sugar and marbles to half fill each of the other pots.

4. Shake each of the pots. Can you tell what is inside it by the sound it makes?

5. Try the test on a friend.

Glossary

chime bar an instrument that makes a note when hit

cymbal an instrument that makes a noise when struck against another cymbal

damage to cause harm

earmuffs pads you put over your ears to keep out sound, or to keep them warm

headphones a device you put over your ears to listen to music, words or other sounds

note a single musical sound

ripple these are tiny up and down movements, like tiny waves in the sea

senses ways of knowing what is happening outside and inside your body. Seeing, hearing, tasting, smelling and touching are the five different senses

sound waves waves that carry sound

vehicle machines that carry people and things from one place to another

Index